Liminal

Liminal

David Bowles

Copyright 2024 @ David Bowles
All-Rights Reserved

ISBN: 978-1-962148-11-5
LOC: 2024940792

Cover Photo:

Lamar University Literary Press
Beaumont, TX

Acknowledgements

Several poems in *Liminal* were previously published in the following journals

F(r)iction Magazine

Fifth Wednesday Journal

Texas Weather (Lamar University Press, 2016)

Voices de la Luna

Imaniman: Poets Writing in the Anzaldúan Borderlands (Aunt Lute, 2016)

Bearing the Mask: Southwestern Persona Poems (Dos Gatos, 2016)

Concho River Review

Amazing Eclectic Anthology (Western Mountain Press, 2016)

Cybersoleil Journal

BorderSenses

Illya's Honey

Red River Review

The Thing Itself

Amarillo Bay

Goodbye, Mexico: Poems of Remembrance (Texas Review Press, January 2015)

Langdon Review of the Arts in Texas

Recent Poetry from Lamar University Literary Press

Lisa Adams, *Xuai*
Walter Bargen, *My Other Mother's Red Mercedes*
Jerry Bradley, *Collapsing into Possibility*
Mark Busby, *Through Our Times*
Julie Chappell, *Mad Habits of a Life*
Stan Crawford, *Resisting Gravity*
Glover Davis, *My Cap of Darkness*
William Virgil Davis, *The Bones Poems*
Jeffrey DeLotto, *Voices Writ in Sand*
Chris Ellery, *Elder Tree*
Dede Fox, *On Wings of Silence*
Alan Gann, *That's Entertainment*
Larry Griffin, *Cedar Plums*
Michelle Hartman, *Irony and Irrelevance*
Katherine Hoerth, *Goddess Wears Cowboy Boots*
Michael Jennings, *Crossings: A Record of Travel*
Gretchen Johnson, *A Trip Through Downer, Minnesota*
Betsy Joseph, *Only So Many Autumns*
Ulf Kirchdorfer, *Chewing Green Leaves*
Jim McGarrah, *A Balancing Act*
J. Pittman McGehee, *Nod of Knowing*
Laurence Musgrove, *Bluebonnet Sutras*
Benjamin Myers, *Black Sunday*
Janice Northerns, *Some Electric Hum*
Godspower Oboido, *Wandering Feet on Pebbled Shores*
Carol Coffee Reposa, *Underground Musicians*
Jan Seale, *The Parkinson Poems*
Steven Schroeder, *the moon, not the finger, pointing*
Glen Sorestad, *Hazards of Eden*
Vincent Spina, *The Sumptuous Hills of Gulfport*
W.K. Stratton, *Betrayal Creek*
Wally Swist, *Invocation*
Ken Waldman, *Sports Page*
Loretta Diane Walker, *Ode to My Mother's Voice*
Dan Williams, *Past Purgatory, a Distant Paradise*
Jonas Zdanys, *The Angled Road*

For information on these and other Lamar University Literary Press books go to www.Lamar.edu/literarypress

CONTENTS

11 That Side

13 Por la libre
14 Border Folk
16 Calendar Round
17 La Calle del Taco
18 Santander
20 Braided Soul
21 The Sea-Ringed World
22 I Once Loved You, Monterrey
24 The Streets of Oaxaca de Juárez
26 Monte Albán
28 Snorkeling at la Entrega
29 Lunch at la Maguey
30 Café Huatulco
31 the bulge and nuzzle of the sea
32 The Trail to Ixchel
34 Familia Dividida

35 This Side

36 Tompakawai Fisherman
37 Borderland Sky
38 The Wall
39 Undocumented
40 Let Me Bury My Son
43 Tlacuache, Cornered
45 Lullaby
44 Beer Bottles
46 The Serpent in My Eye
47 Black Dog
49 Crawlspace
50 The Secret Lives of Numbers
52 Lesson
53 Losing My Accent
54 First Kill
55 The Crockpot
56 Abandoned Anniversary

56	Abandoned Anniversary
59	Fragments of Magic
62	Facing the Tornado
61	Drought
62	Egrets
63	The Falls at Bull Creek
64	Fellowship
65	Grapefruit
66	Dolphin Dreams

67   Liminal Folk

68	To the Little Girl I Can't Quite Recall
69	La Mecánica
71	A Trilingual Elegy for Gloria Anzaldúa
72	Tanka for the Greats
73	Lenguas Despiadadas
74	Escape
86	The Cost of Burning
79	trustee
81	A thing enskied
82	Tessitura
83	La gente en junio
85	Iteration
87	Tzompantli
88	Lovely Thing
89	Ashen Boy
90	Nepantlero

91   Crossing the Threshold

92	Awakening to the Moon
93	Potter at Chaco
94	The Binding of the Years
96	Three Aztec Kings, Cocooned
98	Aztlan Abandoned
100	Pausing to Gaze upon Death's Bleak Spore
101	Marigolds
102	Crow, Buzzard and Hummingbird
104	outside the earthborn brain
105	And on the mere the wailing died away

106	Malinalli Steps into the Gap
107	Night Axe
109	Gonzalo Guerrero
112	The Deep Road

That Side

Por la libre

Just out of Reynosa, you shifted into fifth
And roared to the state line, cigarette in hand.
At the checkpoint we just waved our IDs,
My license, your green card, no need for permits
Or passports then. You pulled into a depósito,
Bought a six-pack of Tecate Light
And then we hit the freeway.
Clutching a can between your knees,
You worked the gearshift like a racer,
Blazing along a thin ribbon of grey
Down that arid, brush-specked plain,
Alejandra Guzmán crooning hoarse against guitars
As I leaned back in the bucket seat, watching you,
The wind snatching at your dark curls,
Rattling your earrings.

I surrendered myself to the speed, to the road,
Utterly in your hands as you blew through Bravo,
The towns of China and Los Ramones a distant blur,
The petroleum fields of Cadereyta belching fire—
Two hundred kilometers in about two hours.
At Guadalupe you looped to skirt Monterrey
Till the Sierra Madre rushed rocky toward us,
The massive "M" of Chipinque verdant with pine.
You downshifted, took us up that sinuous road,
Parked away from other cars. Then hand-in-hand,
Intoxicated by the drive, the music, the beer,
We slipped into those clinquant shadows
Beneath the gnarled and silent boughs
And made love upon the leaves and needles
Like a Huastec couple three millennia past,
Newly arrived in these holy heights,
Having traveled from Mayan lands
To be joined together before the gods
At the very tip of the world.

Border Folk

It was 1983. Saturdays, my dad would rouse me early,
The dawn fumbling blind through the dense south Texas fog,
And we'd drive across the bridge into Nuevo Progreso,
The river roiling and rushing far below.

I was always struck by the skewed sameness,
The familiar differences that tease the mind,
The town a shadow sister of mine and others along the verge
Of here and there, Spanish in mostly all the expected spots,
English missing from official signage but cropping up
Unexpected like hints of jalapeño in the midst of sweetness,
Tourists smiling delighted at the broken but earnest messages
Of curio shops and street vendors, dentists and cops.

We would have breakfast in the same restorán,
Dad sipping café de olla while I drank my chocolate,
Savoring the hints of cinnamon and vanilla,
Sweat beading my face as I ate my huevos rancheros.
We would stroll along the uneven sidewalks, perusing goods,
Dad stopping to chat with strangers or familiar faces,
All of them willing, time-worn greetings and topics interwoven
Into a woof my adolescent eyes could nearly see in the air,
Dense Spanish sparkling with ancient hospitality.
I was the silent güero, pale and freckled, so unlike my darker father,
But my copper hair was tussled all the same.

We would load the car with Mexican cokes and Joya,
So much tastier, more refreshing than American drinks,
Glass bottles tinkling like angel bells,
And driving out to the edge of town to the Pemex station,
We would fill dad's guzzler to the brim with gasoline
Before heading home.

I remember asking once, as he paid the attendant and exchanged a joke,
Why we could speak Spanish despite our surname,
Why all my cousins were Garza and Pérez and Casas,
Why I was cursed to stand out not just because of my Anglo mother
But also because of his imprecise heritage,
A man that straddled ethnicities without a word of explanation.

"We are border folk," he said with a wry grin, "bloodlines
That cross and recross boundaries of river and class and culture.

Each of us is who he is, wholly unique unto himself,
A wondrous admixture of language and tradition.
Do not be ashamed. There is no limit you cannot cross,
For you are frontier-forged."

Now, thirty years later, I traverse that bridge with my own son,
Dark like my father, child of a Mexican mother and this unlikely Chicano.
I pull into a spot along the empty streets, a quick "ahí le encargo"
To the brown-shirted, entrepreneurial, ad-hoc parking attendant.
We walk together into the same eatery. I have coffee, he sips chocolate.
There is a stillness here that worries me, an unraveling of tapestries
That seems to mirror my own losses. On the street, music jangles awkward
Into the emptiness. A few tourists ignore government warnings
And wander like us. Vendors smile and hawk their wares,
Willing to chat though with a forced casualness
That their twitching eyes belie.

My son wants us to hurry. We have come to pick up his glasses.
That is what this place has become for me: cheap medicine and car repair.
The border is diminished, border folk unmoored.
I give the attendant a ten-peso coin.
We drive back in silence.
The river roils, rushes.

Calendar Round

The pharmacist points to the far wall,
Where clay masks and bronze crosses
Hang, statues and alebrijes ranged round
Like mythic sentinels. "I sell those, too."
He tells the winter Texans in proper English
Glazed with a sort of phonological adobo.
The man glances at his wife, then points
To the round Mesoamerican calendar.
"How much for that? The circular stone."
The pharmacist smooths his white coat,
Considers. "Ah, well, I let you have that
For discount price. Just twenty pesos."
I cannot help but ask, looking on at the
Three of them, "¿Por qué tan barato?"
He turns to me with full sincerity.
"It is expired, joven. You have not heard?
The Mayan calendar ended in 2012.
I fear this one is no longer current."
Biting my tongue, I nod and withdraw
So their transaction can conclude.
Above Reynosa's quitting-hour streets
The sun slips down the sky and the
Moon comes over the horizon: I watch
And ponder all the cycles and spirals
Rejected for the straight, unbroken line.

La Calle del Taco

We tumbled from the disco at 3 am,
A gaggle of giggling college students
Months shy of legal, drawn to Mexico.
Yellow street lights and flickering neon
Cast a grimy sheen across near-deserted streets.
A band of mariachis clumped disheveled
In a parking lot, smoking, their instruments strewn.
Down the street, raucous and wild,
Came a knot of grungy punks,
Some as young as thirteen, I'd bet,
Wasted and completely lost. A cop eyed them.
We pointed and guffawed as one girl
Spewed technicolor vomit into a doorway.
Stupid kids. But as they weaved along,
We all tensed up. No reason to, turns out:
The mariachi played them an upbeat song, free,
The transit officer pointed them toward the bridge.

We piled into my car like circus clowns,
But collective antojo pulled the steering wheel
And we wound up on La Calle del Taco,
Where a couple of stands were steaming
With tacos mañaneros, perfect for munchies
And counteracting the inevitable afternoon hangover.
Everyone leaned against the black plastic and steel
Or sat on the hood, soaking their snacks with salsa.
As the less inebriated designated driver, I asked the total.
"Cuarenta," the vendor said. *Forty? Oh, shit.*
I pulled a twenty from my pocket, made a circuit
Of my friends, collecting wrinkled bills and coins
Till I had gathered the sum. I thrust the money
Into his hands, and he blinked for a few seconds.
"No, cuarenta *pesos*, joven." He extracted twelve bucks,
Passed the rest back to me. "Manejen con cuidado."
Less honest, world-wise, good-hearted than he
Or the cop or the mariachis,
I pocketed the money,
For it was my car
And needed gas.

Santander

My younger daughter's burning up
with fever. Careless, unthinking,
I give her a dropper of her sister's
antibiotics. Within minutes, she's
turning purple, her neck swelling
like a goiter, ranine and ominous.
Her breathing is labored, she whines
weakly, she's only a toddler...
I rush to my wife who says
jump in the car, we have to take
her to the emergency room, but
not in the US, she says as she peels
out of the driveway and I clutch
the baby to me, those bastards
don't know what they're doing
y le van a chingar. Thank God
the oldest is with her abuela.
The Reynosa bridge is packed
and we exchange panicked
blame, voices rising as the child
squirms. Then we're through
and she caroms past Los Arcos,
turning left toward Hospital
Santander. I'm opening the door
before she can put the handbrake
on and sprinting to the entrance.
I don't even want to look down,
what if she's dead, what if I'm
holding the cold body of my little
girl and it's all my fault. The nurse
takes her from me, lays her on a
stretcher as I babble an explanation,
my wife too overwhelmed, her role
as driver over. They wheel my baby
off and I twitch with fear that slicks
my hands as I fill out forms. Soon
we just sit together, huddled before
the yawing darkness of uncertainty,
my wife's fingers clutching mine,

no words to say. The doctor emerges
after a time, nodding his head. "She
is allergic to penicillin," he declares.
"Didn't they tell you?" My wife
sighs, grimaces. "American doctors,"
she says simply. "Will she be okay?"
Lucky we brought her so quickly,
near suffocation. Antihistamines
have kicked in. We're to come back
in a few weeks, to his clinic. He'll
do a full study. We pay him, fill
the prescription. My wife cradles
our child as I take my time driving.
I look around at the city, thankful.
I'm a first-year teacher, no insurance
on my family, perhaps irresponsible,
but Mexico, like a spinster aunt
who dabbles in *curanderismo*,
waits to gather her northern nieces
and nephews and kiss the pain away.

Braided Soul

Before the monks came,
the original peoples
had three souls.

Teyolia—to use one of its names—was the spirit,
living on after death, released into paradise
and whatever lies beyond even that unknowable realm.

Ihiyotl was the breath, soul of emotions
and passions, the source of personal magic,
which shamans pooled and channeled.

Tonalli was created upon birth, congealing
from the divine energy that infused blood and brain,
capricious and slippery animal soul, often straying.

The monks shook their heads at this.
"One soul," they instructed. "El ánima.
Deposited in our flesh there in our mother's womb."

And as their culture and faith twist down the years
around those indigenous strands, we mestizo children
nod in growing epiphany sent from Dual God or Trinity—

There has always been one soul, just braided from the three.

The Sea-Ringed World
A paean to Mexico, called Cemanahuac by the ancients

In dreams I see with old eyes
Ancestors prowling
In jaguar pelts and feathers
Upon wooded slopes
Obsidian blades
Clutched like talons in their hands
As they hiss in awe.

In the darkling light they've spied
Towering ghostly
Piercing the very heavens
That sacred ceiba
Axis mundi, the World Tree
And with them I climb
To mist-shrouded, dizzy heights.

Wispy soft and light
As the skirt of Mother God
Comes a cloud of butterflies
Hummingbirds and cotingas
Quetzals and ibis.
They intone the sacred song
And we gasp as we look down.

Caught in the jade-green embrace
of a cosmic sea
Mexico sprawls majestic
Beneath haughty sun
Melancholy sister moon
Four hundred brothers
Slain, transfigured into stars.

When the vision fades
A guttural snarl
Slips my bifurcated tongue
Into the bleak, conquered night:
Mocemanaz Cemānāhuac!
Cemanahuac shall endure!

I Once Loved You, Monterrey

I once loved you, Monterrey—
Your looming, flinty peaks and hills
That slope suggestive, steep and full;
Your ample basin, split in twain
By Catarina's ghostly flow;
Your fringe of forest, dappling stone
As cascades rush headlong
Past grottoes dark and ancient.

I did so love your people,
Their warm embrace, their gentle smile,
Their easy words and open minds,
The food they pressed into my hands,
The simple wisdom of their tales,
The joyful laughter, sprightly dance,
Undaunted spirit, tempered steel.

I even loved your wending streets,
Your grimy shrines to industry,
Your crooked signs and overpasses,
Patchwork sidewalks, leaning fences
Topped with broken glass and wire,
Riotous colors breaking ranks
Here and there amidst the grey,
That mighty square they call your heart,
The cathedral, the fountains, the emerald beam.

But now what villain grips you tight,
What evil worms into your soul?
Lawless brigands blight your beauty,
Carving you into warring claves...
Kidnapped loved ones, severed limbs,
Locked-down schools, journalists slain,
Nightclubs that fester when they're not burning,
Mordidas, corruption, narcocultura,
Chancres that bubble and burst and run.

Oh, I once loved you, Monterrey,
But now I watch you from afar,

How you turn your back on so much history,
Your regal bearing broken, bleeding,
And I hope to see you rise, defiant,
To shrug the demons from your back,
To draw those foothills round your shoulders,
To right the crown of pines upon your brow
And urge me to your side, dear queen.

The Streets of Oaxaca de Juárez

Along the banks of the Atoyac
the white spheres of guaje blooms
dip in humble welcome.
Ahead the city sprawls to vibrant life,
accreted in kludgy layers down the millennia,
wending willy-nilly across the valley floor.
Sweep down its narrow streets of stone and tar:
noise roils like a tangible cloud—music and horns
and shouts and the distant boom of mines
yielding only stubbornly the gold and silver
Cortés came to steal. Pungent smells curl round
and envelope: chocolate, chiles,
smoke, mescal, tropical blooms.

But the city of Benito Juárez is not buildings,
sound, aromas—the people smile and hug
and melodically speak of their wares,
their lives, their history. They are Oaxaca.
Artisans who carve many-hued alebrijes
to stave off nightmares, chocolatiers who
crush almonds and cinnamon and sugar
into the dark grains of cacao grounds,
vendors of stone replicas of Zapotec gods
and painted tin crosses and baskets,
jewelry, earthenware, worm salt,
grilled grasshoppers, bright blouses
and skirts and boots and belts....

The food. Divine. The seven mole sauces,
thick and nuanced. Tlayudas, piled high
with beans and meat and cheese.
Aguas frescas and nieves to stave off
the tropical heat. Black beans and tamales
redolent of exotic epazote and pitonia.
Deep draughts from bowls of aguamiel
or thick, brothy tejate, a meal in itself.

The sun sinks down the sky, silhouetting Fortin Hill
and Monte Albán against lurid mauve and pale blue.

If the city was vibrant during the day, the evening
starts it swirling. Down the cobbled streets
to the Zócalo, vast arbored square girded by
arched and spanned colonial structures,
flows a flood of music and dance and spectacle,
writhing and joyous. Zandungas and jarabes,
pirouetting chinas and prancing papier-mâché
calendas. Declaimed poetry, street theater,
human statues amid the throb of pre-Colombian beats.

Into the wee hours the revelry waxes and wanes
till for brief span all is quiescent under mother moon
and four hundred southern stars. Then, like a silent,
holy gift, the sun lifts golden plumes over the mountains,
illuminating the Cathedral of Our Lady of the Assumption,
hewn from what seem living blocks of verdant cantera
for which the city is called *la Verde Antequera*,
a green that appears to bleed into the water,
threading up into the emerald foothills
of the Sierra Madre del Sur, past mighty Monte Albán,
sustained—the ancients say—by the lingering life-force
of the kind and gentle Zapotec princess Donají,
beheaded near the margins of the Atoyac River
when she sued her people's enemies for peace.

Monte Albán

Beneath the clear, warm skies of southern Mexico,
our bus groans up the twisting single lane,
swerving nauseously close to sheer drops,
outstripping the urban sprawl that clings like lichen.
Then bright, loud Oaxaca falls away at last,
and the road wends soft and sinuous into lush woods.

We disembark, greeted by the calls of flocking vendors
and guides. My wife haggles the price of stone figurines
while I shop for hats to shield against the winter sun.
A short walk, and there before us spread the ruins—
a vast, majestic city erected two millennia ago
on a ridge flattened by Zapotec hands.

Ambling past the ball court where players once
used hips and yokes to fling rubber spheres
through stone rings, we descend into the plaza,
a vast green field lined by palaces and temples.
Awestruck, I whisper of thick throngs that teemed
in these broad, grassy avenues—bustling markets.

Southward sits an altar, partly recessed. We imagine
lying there, awaiting the sacrificial knife, blue-spangled
heavens looming in welcome. Beyond the temple
stands the observatory, cater-cornered jarringly
in violation of the religious regularity of the site,
oriented to the higher science of the stars.

In the shadow of the towering South Platform,
we curve northward, passing the Danzantes,
those contortionists carved into stone whose dance
is in truth the final, frantic throes of death.
We rest on stone benches, beneath the broad boughs
of trees, and look upon the palaces with sober eyes.

Then up the steep steps of the North Platform to stare
down into the Sunken Patio and its obscure altar, place
of hidden rites, climbing higher, mounting the ziggurat
to gaze trembling at the massive expanse of white and

gray stone against emerald, once home to tens of thousands, master of leagues and leagues of land. Now empty. Silent.

From the mists of the past, a blood-curdling scream rings out. I shudder and turn to see my son standing between two plinths, arms outstretched, head lolling, transfixed against the heavens. Caught in the moment, I rush to his side. He winks and smiles. "I'd make a good victim, wouldn't I?" he quips. I force a laugh, but I cannot help thinking of all the altars he may not escape.

Snorkeling at la Entrega

water clear as untrammeled mountain lakes,
warm, embryonic, enfolding head and limbs,
only sound the ebb and flow of waves
(mother's heartbeat thrumming through the world)
yes, and the raspy spit of even breath.

as the beach recedes, a cooler current—
what a cosmos opens there below!
darting luminescence, scales that gleam,
startling, eldritch hues that twist the mind,
spines and stars and undulating trees.

near the mouth of the bay, the Pacific verge,
caverns await, half submerged like traps.
enter like a pilgrim, humble and slow:
then the everlasting suck and surge—
mighty respiration of the sea.

Lunch at la Maguey

There's a gazebo
of palm fronds and sturdy wood
on nearly white sand.
Waiter takes our mackerels,
promises four whole dishes.

We seize coconuts,
take deep draughts to quench the thirst
of hours on the sea.
Nearby, 80s tunes are sung
in samba-beat Portuguese.

The breeze has dried us
by the time they bring our food—
dark meat basted slow.
We remember our promises
and waste not a single bite.

Sated, we just watch
the turquoise waves lap the shore
like tongues of maguey,
sinking into the silence
of comfort and family.

Café Huatulco

In the center of Huatulco, near the bay,
Where picturesque and cobbled streets debouche,
Ensconced in shady trees that mask the quay,
A kiosk nestles, welcoming and hushed.

Come sit at rough-hewn tables and delight
In cups of liquid magic, shaman brew!
Such coffee masters taste and smell and sight—
It reaches deep and fills you, soul and thew.

Ah, whence the bean that gladdens tourists' hearts?
Plantations in those mountains, green and cool,
That rise above the sea. The breeze imparts
Uncommon taste. Native hands work the soil.

The owners grind it fine and pour your cup,
Then raise their own in honest fellowship.

the bulge and nuzzle of the sea

narrow crescent of beach
tumbled into being by
the lightest of tremors,
a shuddering lover's touch,
Playa Fandango cleaves to the cliff
silvered virginal by stars and moon.

wending down precarious ledges,
through darkling fronds and ferns,
we emerge upon the pebbly strand
and kneel silent in the shallows—
the Pacific draws away, then resumes
his slow caress, keening muted passion.

The Trail to Ixchel
At the edge of the ruins of Uxmal in Yucatán

The legend tells that the Dwarf King,
after winning the throne ten centuries past
from a cruel and selfish despot,
built a home for his mother, the Witch
(humble and nondescript, at her request)
near the forest's looming edge.

And as I stand here penitent
amid the rubble that remains,
wondering at her motives
in rejecting all that wealth,
a narrow path draws my eye
into the gloomy wood.

Compelled by what I cannot say,
I enter that hushed and verdant
realm, the leaves beneath my feet
untrodden for months, I judge.
Ducking under branches, leaping
over fallen trees, I venture deep.

Though my pace is quick, the way
wends on and on, farther and farther
from the bustle of murmuring tourists
till I almost falter and turn back,
afraid of dusk and denizens unseen,
something subtle shifting in the green.

The path crests a sort of hill above
vine-crusted ruins. There I'm stopped
by a silence so thick and absolute
it thrums in my very bones
till overcome with startled awe
I fall to my knees in surrender.

A corroded sign tells me this is her temple:
Ixchel, Lady Rainbow, fierce and aged goddess
of fertility and war, of shamans and medicine.

I need no guide to expound upon her might—
beside that shattered stone yawns a pit
from which ancient sounds creak and flit.

The wind hushes round, a probing caress,
and I feel my soul laid bare to her gaze:
all my doubts and sins, fragility and flaws.
I begin to weep, hoarse and raw, openly
broken at long last—and the canopy echoes
with caws and howls and rattling limbs.

How to describe such a trick of the mind?
My agnostic heart, so lost in the dark,
for a fleeting moment in that primal shrine
feels the healing touch of the quiet divine.

Familia Dividida
The Río Grande River between Paso Lajitas and Lajitas, 2015

Saraí rushes the water
like it's the Jordan,
amid the thronging surge
of weeping, laughing souls.

Doña Chata squints rheumy eyes,
skirts gathered to her knee.
She glimpses Saraí, notes
braids rimed with unexpected age,
the older
plunges headlong
heedless of muddy spray.

Madre e hija collide,
euphoric embrace
between here
and allá,
more than a decade of separation
dissolving into tears.

Repeating up and down
this stretch of the Río Grande—
two communities, two countries,
once weft and warp of love and tradition,
a vibrant fabric,
razor wires now partition:
hate and fear and politics.

For an hour,
watched through glinting scopes
from rumbling jeeps,
this divided family is whole

like a lost soul dipped
beneath redeeming waters
while a dove croons idyllic peace
upon a broken sunbeam.

This Side

Tompakawai Fisherman

The barrel cactus all abloom,
kissed beautiful by Father Sun,
I whisper a prayer to Mother Earth and wade
into the shallows of the oxbow lake.

Light I heft my spear, carved careful
from a thick but supple branch of wild olive
as I rested in the ebony and brasil shade
over a week of midday heat.

Down my forearm an alligator creeps,
writhing as my muscles tense
ink blending with my blood to give me strength,
precision, make my aim true.

From all around come the call of the green jay
and the chattering chachalaca. The ragged growls
of jaguarundis and ocelots echo in the undergrowth—
the snarling solidarity of hunters.

And then, a flash of silver. The spear leaps
from my hand, guided by lore, ancestors,
the will of gods themselves. A burst of cloudy red
and I lift the fish free, a gift of shimmering wriggles.

I murmur my thanks to our Mother for waters
that sustain us, and clean my catch,
offering entrails in silent homage to Father Sun
before wrapping the flesh in pungent leaves.

My children will eat well today,
This iridescence roasted into smiles.

Borderland Sky

endless, blue so hot it edges
toward white, pitiless,
indifferent to the flat coastal
plain, dots of grey-bottomed
and alluring wet harried by
the gulf's gusting breath—
meager, fleeting shadows
on the brown brush, the
turgid, wild river below.

or black, a sable cape slowly
bangled with glinting silver,
flung over the eyes of the
wide world to calm its
snorting rage, but ominous
and hinting at bleak endings,
raked at breath-taking
moments by the death
of blazing stars, tumbling.

behold its denizens, legends
in flight—the cruel lechuzas,
witches feathered by blackest night
snatching naughty children
from homey bosoms;
the Big Bird, its prehistoric
and craggy features snarling
like a crazed ape as it dips
its leathery wings our way;

la Llorona, drifting over
water, moaning for her
children, dragging
stragglers into the depths—
all the harpies, lost souls,
thunderbirds and legless
vampires of lore, criss-
crossing that vastness,
looking down at us.

The Wall

Small minds love lines,
straight-edged and two-dimensional,
slashed through sand or upon maps,
starkly marking this and that.

Small minds see barriers in nature,
bark of tree, rind of fruit,
skin and fur and water's edge:
as soon as they can, they lift their own
with nimble little monkey hands.

But barriers are permeable:
deserts comingle with forests,
flora flourish in our guts,
and even minds bleed across the ether.

The wall stands, a gash
in the porous membrane of millennia,
yet birds still wing their journeys above,
water and root curl beneath,
and wind rattles its laughing way through the bars.

How foolish to expect that such a flimsy thing
could ever stop the flow of dreams, ideas, or love.

Undocumented
Overheard at a construction site in the Rio Grande Valley

There on the roof you'll see my illegals,
Putting down tar paper for the shingles
Or tiles, I forget which. Hardworking? Yup.
Most have families to feed, and bills keep
Coming. I pay them fifty bucks a day,
A hell of a lot more than nothing, guy.
Well, sure, some do complain, the typical
Rabble-rousing bastards who just don't feel
They're being given a fair shake. This one
Snooty beaner, an engineer back home,
Thought he'd organize the crew, make demands.
I fired the whole lot, called up a friend
On the Border Patrol, got them thrown out
Of the country. Some were back at the site
Within a week, heads hanging low, begging
For me to take them on again. "Sure thing,"
Says I. "But it's thirty-five dollars now."
And they stayed, working hard! Just goes to show:
I'd given that sumbitch my confidence,
Figured an engineer would be of use.
Hell, I was going to raise his pay clear
Up to eighty, make him an overseer.
Uppity shit bit the hand that fed him.
I heard he had crossed again; I for damn
Sure wasn't going to let him work, though:
I called all the contractors that I know
And burned him real good. Doors shut on his face.
You know how it is. Got to learn their place.
A pool, you say? Other crew works cement.
Here's some photos: cribbed the plans from the Net.

Let Me Bury My Son
Near Brownsville, 1915

On my knees I beg for the love of God:
Mister Lawman, let me bury my son.

They say he's a traitor, bandit, thief:
My boy was only working at his uncle's side.

We said nothing when your people took our land,
Bought up our ranches, pushed us south of town.

We cast our eyes aside, picked up spade and hoe
To work the soil where once our cattle grazed.

Don't strip this final dignity away, good sir:
Mister Lawman, let me bury my son.

All of you afraid of that plan
Hatched by rebels to cut you down as one

This isn't Mexico. We're Tejanos, faithful
To our state. We seek no revolution.

Federal troops and Rangers far outnumber
These brown-skinned, Spanish-tongued neighbors.

A train has been derailed, I know. Bandits
Bolted back across the Río Grande.

In rage the troops returned to find my son at work
With his uncle and others on one of your farms.

Those calloused hands, would they ever
Lift a rifle, ever curl around your neck?

My son's hands, even free of dirt, are not
White. Evidence enough for you. Each hanged—

A mother's grief at the loss of her son—
Bereft, I traveled to that tall, bleak mesquite

Wept to see my brother dead, howled to see my son.
Rangers laughed. They would not let me cut him down.

His limbs swelled tight against his clothes.
They would not let me cut him down.

The sun beat down and blacked his flesh.
They would not let me cut him down.

The flies like smoke then wreathed him dark.
They would not let me cut him down.

The vultures swarmed and pecked and tore.
They would not let me cut him down.

Still he sways from that noose, creaking in the wind.
There are rites we must perform—our God commands.

Think of all these spirits, curdling in shame,
Think of vengeance brewing slow in the sandy soil.

Show me that you're human. Even now there's time.
By everything that's holy: let me bury my son.

Tlacuache, Cornered

Once revered,
the opossum crouches
hissing
indignant
in the cobwebby darkness
beneath the mobile home.
Lizards scatter scurrying
at the sibilant sound and
at the eyes glowing green
that steadily approach.

The cat is an intruder
a mercenary
cold and calculating
clawed and swift
that does not belong
brought like smallpox
and steel to this world
to wreak death upon birds
and fallen kings.

For the opossum ruled
when man was young
and gave him fire
and fermented drink
and was ever treated
with dignity. But here
among sloshing pipes
ragged insulation
oblivious anthills
he makes his last
desperate
stand.

Lullaby

For border babes the dark descends
A few days after birth:
Cradled in abuela's arms,
They learn that danger lurks.

Duérmete mi niño
Duérmeteme ya
Porque viene el Cucu
Y te comerá.

As they grow, the boogeymen
Will multiply and spread
Until at last not even sleep
Can keep those maws away.

Y si no te come,
Él te llevará
Hasta su casita
Que en el monte está.

They'll watch their friends get dragged into
That lair of smothered dreams
And learn at last the Cucu thrives
Within the hearts of men.

Beer Bottles

My grandfather
Manny Garza
Had three loves:
Golf, beer, and
Green-eyed girls
(Hence his marriage
To my grandmother
And their later divorce).
But of these three,
The greatest was beer.

When I was barely a toddler
He'd drive up to Corpus
To visit and fish.
He and Dad would pack me up
Along with the cooler and gear,
And we'd drive to the beach.
They'd fish while I fiddled with sand,
Watching a wall of glass bottles
Slowly erect itself along the shore.

When the fish weren't biting,
It amused Manny to no end
To pour beer into a baby bottle
And give it to me. The first time,
I scrunched my face up
At the taste, but sipped again.
His laughter was louder
Than the surf, startling.

This happened every time he visited.
I never cried, though.
Instead, as he mocked me one day,
I discovered a clever trick:
Shaking the bottle with all my might
Till the fizzy froth pushed
Against my stubby little hands,
I pressed my finger against the nipple
And sent a stream arcing through the air

That got him in the eye,
Ending my precocious binge.

The Serpent in My Eye

I still recall the day
it uncoiled its glassy shaft
upon the world
as I dashed down the alley—
a crooked snake that twined
at the edge of things,
floating away from my focus,
haloed by strange, transparent bubbles.

I was five. It seemed a sign
from the unknowable vastness,
a mark or brand, a dark sigil,
companion along a sinful road.
The viper never left.
It burrowed.

Ten years later I learned
its names: *myodesopsia*.
Musca volitans. Floaters
Made stark by astigmatism.
But by then the wyrm
was curling in dark corners
of my soul,
well beyond the reach
of corrective lenses,
scalpels,
lasers.

Black Dog

Come quick, the neighbor kid said.
Your brother. A big dog has him.

I rushed out of the duplex where
I was playing, a simple pre-fab
affair that smelled of bologna,
kool-aid and pee, like most of the
homes on that Texas naval base.

The buildings were arranged
in a semi-circle, with a broad
communal yard that seemed a park
to my five-year-old perspective.

There you lay beneath an ash,
little brother, not quite three.
Above you stood a massive
black dog, female, dugs hanging
low enough to graze your head.

She was growling, teeth bared,
while you played with a toy car.

Grown-ups kept creeping close,
but the bitch would snarl and bark,
snapping her foam-flecked teeth
as if you were her pup, your life
dependent on her protection.

And here the memory fades,
goes hazy. A part of me knows
that Dad or someone managed
to get you free. In deeper layers
of my mind, I walk up to the dog
and speak to her softly till she leaves
to grieve elsewhere for her lost babies.
But you and I know both versions are lies,
little brother. No one ever got you free.
She looms above you still, does she not,

her jaws slavering, rumbling rabid,
keeping the universe at bay.

Crawlspace

When we moved into the parsonage,
I climbed up onto a chair to slide my box
of prized comics onto the wooden shelf
in my closet and discovered a hidden panel.
Behind it lay a twisting crawlspace that led
from room to room, closet to closet.

For weeks I shimmied and skittered
through the ducts of a government lab,
the bowels of an alien spaceship,
the vermin-infested tunnels of trolls.
I overheard their chittering, complex tongue
and came to slow, silent understanding.

The secrets gnawed at my mind. I twitched
with the need to let their victims know
of those nefarious and nebulous plans.
A long-haired, doe-eyed convert smiled
at me one Sunday. I couldn't help whispering
"My parents say you'll fall off the wagon."

Stupid. Of course the brain-washed zombie
would hurry to them, hoping to curry favor.
The crawlspace was nailed shut. I was hung
on a rack of cleverly encoded bible verses
until my weak, submissive heart seemed broken.
They hadn't noticed the gap in the skirting

looming with sly promise
beneath the back porch.

The Secret Lives of Numbers

When I was very young, I could not grasp
the cold certainty of numbers. I saw faces
in the world, personalities carved like Shinto
gods in rock, river, and rail. I understood
people, not abstractions. Frustrated, I snarled
at the ordered row of digits till they bowed
and showed me their true natures.

1, 2 and 3 were brothers, each older than
the last. While they all loved one another,
1 and 2 were closest. 3, tougher and more
mature, loved and was loved by 4. Their
romance was happy, lucky, pure.

4's older brother was 5, a serious and steady
chap who liked things ordered and neat.
Strangely, he was best friends with 6,
a rebel among numbers, wild and uncouth.
His dangerous nature drew 7 to him,
that gorgeous, slender princess of the straight
diadem. Their love was doomed by nefast
sums of beauty, beast and her father's rage.

For 8 was an angry man, rich and powerful,
his superiority to lesser numbers countered
by the humiliation he suffered in private,
the two views of himself cycling endlessly.
It was haughty 9, imperious and regal and
all things cold and queenly, who crushed
8's ego as she did all single digits she touched,
decreasing and doubling them in a mockery
of their nature and their love. 7 she would
make 16 for a time, keeping her child from
that peon while sneering and laughing
at his apparent yet impotent presence.

One number she would never approach, however:
the young beatific 1, who quivered at the edge
of nothing and did not go mad. With a smile

he had once embraced 9 and not been diminished.
Instead, the queen had fallen into the circular
abyss, silently screaming until he released her...

Lesson

A circular pool,
Center deeper than edges,
Dark and menacing—
Father hurls me to its heart,
Stares as I struggle to swim.

Losing My Accent

Freshly arrived in McAllen, Texas, my parents'
hometown, I learned that I had an accent.
Kids in class couldn't seem to understand
my South Carolinian draw, the dropped Rs and
lazy dipthongs, much too lethargic to blend.
I knew I would have to make some changes,
but didn't want to sound like cousins and peers,
their short, Tex-Mex vowels, soft Gs and Ps,
devoiced final consonants and popping Vs.
So I studied TV newsmen, reporters, anchors,
the announcers and commercial actors,
and with a summer's practice I ground
my twang into a barely perceptible hint—
the lightest of lilts. When school began again,
I greeted classmates with neutral Midwestern
plainness. "Where you from? ¿D'ónde eres?"
the other kids asked me. But I was no longer
certain, had scoured the South from my tongue,
had refused the spice of my father's culture.
"Nowhere," I blandly muttered. "Everywhere."

First Kill

Anointed with deer blood
by hard men of the bayou
my father became a master hunter.

And since I was his eldest son,
he sought to apprentice me
to rifle and knife and silent death.

He led me into coastal woods
beside cotton-mouth swamps
down shadow-dappled paths

Till we saw a flash of movement
in the gnarled boughs. His nod
told me to raise my sights.

Target practice had carved the habit
into mind and muscle—butt to shoulder,
eye glaring down the barrel, finger taut.

A fleet squirrel stopped and turned.
I squeezed. It fell and lay among the dead
leaves and flat-capped destroying angels.

It was twitching, clinging to life.
"Put it out of its misery," my father said,
so I pointed my rifle at its round, blue eye,

Which looked up at me wetly, almost pleading.
I shut both my own and fired, a sob hitching
my chest. I turned away. I could hear

My father calling me as I dropped the gun
and hurried back through looming oaks
that bent their mossy beards in hate.

The Crockpot

Mother, I know you meant well,
Packing the little crockpot tight
With chunks of potato, whole carrots,
A slab of meat, a random bouillon cube.
You couldn't be home to cook a meal
And food stamps only stretch so far.

But when my brothers and I would tumble
From that hot, oppressive bus
To find your single-mom stew awaiting us,
We learned first-hand the simple bliss
Of bologna, government cheese and *pan Bimbo*—
Sharing a bowl of chips and salsa
On the steps of that housing complex
That roiled with the poorly seasoned smells
Of unattended youth.

Abandoned Anniversary

Thirty-three years later
And your face is blurred
By the darkened glass
Of hardship and oblivion,
Save for flashes in the features of my brother,
Whose soul you dragged away.

Thirty-three years later
And your voice is mere harmonics
Skittering through my songs and poems,
Stripped of accent and con-man smarm,
Undertones in the deepening laugh
Of my son, whom you'll never know.

Thirty-three years later
And you've become a shadowy bulk
That slinks into nightmares
Like you did that last morning
Retrieving your belt buckle from my room
As if taking my name, my birthright.

Thirty-three years later
And I can remember with indelible clarity
The sight of my mother in the breezeway
When I rode my bike up to the complex,
Her face red and haggard from weeping,
Certain you were gone for good.

Thirty-three years later
And the overwhelming silence of abandonment
Still looms bleakly in sealed-off,
Empty halls of my heart,
Those dusty and unused chambers
That once belonged to a father.

Fragments of Magic

Christmas Eve on the border,
unusually hushed and cold.
My house stands festooned
with lights amid the throng
of grapefruit trees, ruby red.

Festivities have wound down;
my nieces sprawl in abandon
on sofas and floor, their parents
nodding off as Miracle on 34th Street
drones quiet and ever-magic.

I step into the kitchen for a drink,
when a glint like alkaloid sand
catches my eye through the window.
I press my face against the pane,
eyes widening with giddy surprise.

No hesitation. I don't call my wife.
I don't wake my sister-in-law or
my brother. I head to my son's room.
The boy is lost in sleep, but my voice,
gentle yet thrilled, stirs him awake:

"Hush, son. Come outside to see
a gift like none you've been given:
pure joy, scattered down from above."
I bundle him up, guide him drowsy,
and then I open wide the door—

The world has been dusted white.
Christmas snow, the kind I've yearned
to touch for more than thirty years.
With crunching steps I lead the way,
whispering to him in awed delight.

"See how the snowflakes drift down,
kissing soft, like icy stars that speck the black?
They're fragments of magic, lovely boy,

heaven dust, blessings shaken out upon
your head by the vast cosmos itself."

Ah, he's only three, but he comprehends.
My words are superfluous. We stand
silent for a moment, the house holy
in its robe of snow, the trees pale
sentinels beneath the clouds.

Then we tumble back upon the ermine
pulled loose over crabgrass and sage,
and for a moment we are angels,
laughing and innocent as we spread
our silver wings upon the earth.

Facing the Tornado

The hurricane lumbered toward us,
a vast, ineluctable force.
Peering through the tempered glass
of our forged metal door,
I glimpsed a portentous movement
and dashed out, nauseous and breathless,
to better scan the clouds.

There it was, that tell-tale swirl,
like serpents curling
in the black guts of the sky.

I grabbed the portable TV,
lamp, blankets, food—
pulled my children and wife
into the hall bathroom,
cinderblock heart of our home,
sanctuary against the growling storm.

We lined the bathtub with bedspreads
and pillows, nestled the little ones in,
made it a game, sang songs against
the whistle and whine and creaking groan.
I kept one eye on the flickering screen,
violent and bloody cells of force
blotting the map by degrees.

I hid my fear from them, but I was vigilant—
divided, letting danger eat me
with a smile and a laugh,
ready to shield them with my flesh
should the heavens spin hungry vipers
toward the fragile rooftop.

Sleep overtook them, in tub and on tiles.
I waited until the eye had passed,
then I too left the dangerous waking world.
In the morning, we arose to a sun that shone
upon a swampy yard. I checked the news.

The tornado had finally touched down
a bit to the northwest of us,
near the empty expressway. Little harm.
We only lost a few shingles. Light debris.

Minor changes, easily erased.
Then I saw the look in my children's eyes
as they hurried to help me,
the pride on their mother's face—
I was more, now, than I had been.

Oh, we all knew deep down
that I can't stave off the dark coils
when they at last choose to strike...
but I made the dreadful bearable
and they loved me for it.

Drought

A white sun peers down
from amongst racing black clouds—
coin-toss of the gods.

Egrets

Beside a canal
Egrets flash white on green weeds—
Harbingers of heat.

The Falls at Bull Creek

There
where the cascade
slaps against
the moss-mottled rocks
bubbles break into being
coruscating silver
upon the stream
buoyed beautiful
for mere moments
till they burst
into water
and air.

Fellowship

Joined in the sizzle, the bubble, the creak,
fanning the coals to candent heat,
thrumming and stamping that quicken the pulse,
hands that thrust aside the ice,
laughter that curls and wreathes like smoke,
flipping and sipping and gnawing the gristle,
stories that simmer and soak in the sun,
drawing the bodies and minds alike
closer together, mortar and pestle,
grinding all cares into piquant fun.

Grapefruit
a mondōka

Ruby red blossoms—
their aroma hinting at
luscious flesh beneath the rind.

Would you press your mouth
against this ripening flesh?
Expect a bittersweet flood.

Dolphin Dreams

Find yourself in awed amazement,
Standing at the river's edge—
Waves that lull you to the water
Ghostly forms that leap and dive.

Body still amidst the breakers,
Mind submerged beneath the foam,
Feel the cosmos drifting nearer,
Bleeding through these dolphin dreams.

Fins that slice through clinquant currents,
Tails that spiral dolphins down,
Jubilant and keenly chirping,
To those blue and glowing depths.

Fathoms deep the dance is wending,
Ancient music billows slow.
Rising now, your soul is bursting,
Yearning toward that distant sun.

Mass of bubbles, fleet crescendo,
Orbiting your morphing form—
With your school you break the surface,
Wakened by these dolphin dreams.

Dolphin dreams can shape your thinking,
Dolphin dreams reflect the light,
Dolphin dreams are full of wonder,
Dolphin dreams will wake the world.

Liminal Folk

To the Little Girl I Can't Quite Recall

Like a bright smear in darkling mists of memory
I can almost see you standing, hip cocked,
laughing as I strike some noble pose.
For the space of a single summer
nearly forty years gone
we spun a wholly new world
culled from comics and pulp novels—
secret African princes, orphaned heiresses,
international intrigue played out
across our military home, a naval base
we traversed on bikes that doubled
as steamers and horses and private jets.
We got lost in each other's minds,
make-believe spinning glittering threads
that bound us in such an inextricable web
that even though I don't remember your face
or your name, there's a sweet glowing hole
in the center of my aging self
that still retains your shape.

La Mecánica

Since she was only four, Papá would perch her
on a side panel, and she would peer
into the complex guts of the engine
as he bent his head beneath the hood
and thrust his hands like a doctor
into the pipes and wires.

Since her brothers were grown, it wasn't long
before he started barking orders at her,
ready to strike if she brought the wrong tool.
Still, he was surprised six years later
to hear that quiet voice mutter
"así no" beside him.

"What did you say?" She pointed at the pulleys.
"You're threading the belt wrong, Papá."
"¡Huerca igualada! Get inside and help your mother
make tortillas!" A shove to punctuate.
But through the kitchen window, she watched
as he pulled the belt free and redid the work.

Little by little he began to call her outside
whenever vexed by a mechanical conundrum.
"What do you think?" he'd ask, and her eyes
would unfailingly diagnose the problem.
He set her to work, finally, taking engines apart,
rebuilding them with such finesse they seemed new.

Men, however, are driven by inscrutable motors.
Diabetes and then renal failure claimed Papá.
She was a teen, and no one would bring work.
No men wanted the scrawny tomboy at their shops,
touching their cars with her nimble fingers.
She had been saving money, though. It was time.

It took her three tries to cross the border. Sent back
twice before she found willing allies in Lopezville
who rented her a little room. Came a day when
their car broke down and they despaired

at the probable cost. She asked to take a look,
unpacked her precious tools, and fixed it for free.

Word spread. The work began to trickle in. A car
every two weeks, then one a week, then more.
She bought a little quarter-acre lot, put a battered
mobile home on it. Soon there was enough to erect
a laminate roof for shade, and her business boomed.
La mecánica, folk called her in a mix of humor and awe.

Bush expanded amnesty in 1990. Her many clients
were now contacts. She got together the documentation
needed, became a permanent resident. Finally returned
to visit her mother, to whom she'd been sending generous
remesas, driving a nearly new sports car she'd souped-up.
Friends and neighbors, once dubious, became obsequious.

At her father's grave, she knelt and laid a gleaming wrench
in lieu of flowers. "Hey, Papá," she muttered. "Next week
construction begins on my shop. No more shade-trees.
Going to realize your dream at last. What do you think
of your tomboy now?" There was no answer, of course—
just the smell of grease and the curves of her waiting wheels.

A Trilingual Elegy for Gloria Anzaldúa

I. tonihtauhca nepantlah

nicān in nepantlahtli
in tlāltzontli ānepantlah
īnepantlah in tlālticpac
huel īyōllo in ilhuicatl
nepanotl titotlahpaloah
iccemmaniyān.

II. Nuestra Gloria en medio

aquí en este lugar de en medio
esta frontera entre las aguas
en el centro de la tierra
en el mismo corazón del cielo
nos abrazamos el uno al otro
para siempre.

III. Our Glory in the Middle / Our Gloria, in Nepantla

here in this middle place
this border in the water's midst
in the center of the earth
at the very heart of heaven
we embrace one another
forever.

Tanka for the Greats
masters of RGV letters

I. *Américo Paredes*

On the battlefield
in Japan, keen reporter
who questioned Tojo—
even then your mestizo pen
bridged cultures near Shinto shrines.

II. *Rolando Hinojosa*

From your mind they flow—
river through Belken County,
chain of mythic towns,
hidden, bicultural history
in voices so real they startle.

III. *Carmen Tafolla*

Just a few years here,
enriching Valley culture,
but your voices echo still—
activist, scholar, and always
la poeta de la gente.

IV. *Jan Seale*

Marriage brought you here,
but the music of the river
mingled with your soul.
Oh! the verses that sprouted—
lovely, verdant and wise.

Lenguas Despiadadas

In a typical South Texas department store
With haughty disdain and arching eyebrows
A *regiomontana* refugee approaches the checkout area
Where Tony "el Lefty" is talking
To his wife on the phone.
"*'Ta bien,* shorty. *Ahí te wacho* in a while."

Under her breath the woman mutters,
"*Lo que más extraño es un español bien hablado.*"
Tony blows a raspberry.
"*Qué naco,*" she sneers
As she cuts in line.
"*Pinche fresa,*" he spits,
Giving her the finger.
"Love Mexico so much?
Pos vete pa'trás."

The exchange degenerates quickly
Into chaos.
Soon most of the customers
Enter the fray, shouting.

Meanwhile, two old men,
A taciturn former *bracero*
And a Winter Texan,
Exchange knowing looks
And move surreptitiously
To the front.

Escape

Don Moncho chafes at the cordial confinement
Of his daughter and son-in-law's middle-class home,
So different from his accustomed abode: never
A house, though he has owned several,
But instead the sinuous arms of the road.

Diabetes unchecked has claimed a kidney,
So now, apart from hospital visits
For debilitating hemodialysis,
He speaks to no one, spends his days
Peering with failing eyes at bible and TV.

One day he can stand no more the muffled
Hum of the air conditioning, the distant
Rattle of passing cars upon the farm road:
Taking up scriptures and useless spectacles
And magnifying glass, he begins to walk.

The winds of the past seem to bear him forward:
He remembers being Raymond, as Nebraskans
Called him in their low, casual voices.
He spent the Korean War in America,
Fixing cars and pleasing women.

But drink and brawling nearly did him in,
So he returned to wife and children
And followed his younger brother into Christ.
El Hermano Ramón could barely read,
But he let the Word lead him through ranches.

Traveling evangelist and mechanic, he made
Little money: his children had to fend
For themselves and for their mother
During his long months in the mountains
Till God told him to found a church.

The reverend now roamed from home to home,
Tending to his needy flock, retiring
Each night to a bed on the rooftop, sprawled

Beneath the beautiful expanse of stars
Laid like a royal highway into the heavens,

The very same path he had studied as a boy,
Herding goats across the vastness of the ranch,
Days without a sign of man's foolishness,
His pointless gouging at earth and sky:
The only company some passing vaquero.

The roar of the expressway reaches him
In the midst of this reverie: he squints and ambles
Under the overpass to reach the store,
Where he asks for a quarter and calls a pastor
Who just might give him a ride to the church.

As he waits near the payphone, a form
Blurry and dark, like some dread apparition,
Wavers its way out of the haze, looming—
A familiar voice scolds him with maternal sting:
His daughter, come to return him to his cell.

The Cost of Burning
a chōka

He's my right-wing friend,
puts god and family first

He loves his country,
the flag, all it represents

A decent man, see?
Latino-values patriot.

But the radicals
have dug their hooks into him

Now he rails against
all the ghostly leftist threats

Whipped into a froth
by those tea-party witch hunts

Spouting sheer nonsense,
like how the Founding Fathers

Wanted a Christian
nation, evangelicals

Inspired by God.
He clings to this fantasy.

I am reminded
of that Mexica ruler

King Itzcoatl,
founder of the Aztec realm.

Throwing off the yokes
of Tepanec overlords
He heeded the words
his nephew Tlacaelel

Uttered in counsel:
"Let us burn the ancient books

Gather every one,
Set our history alight.

It is not wise, King,
that our people know the truth

How the Mexica
scrounged and bartered and begged life

How we sold ourselves
and then slaughtered our masters

How we stole their gods,
their culture, their poetry

And mingled our flesh
with the flesh of their daughters.

Nomads from the wastes,
we have risen to power.

Now we must rewrite
our lowly, ignoble past."

The books of bark burned;
new chronicles were painted.

Those who knew the truth
fell silent or were silenced.

One generation
and the past was forgotten.
Huitzilopochtli,
their god of war, had led them

Out of old Aztlan
south through the wild to that isle.

Eagle, cactus, snake—
they named him God of the Sun

Set him above all,
spread state-sanctioned religion

Fought great Flower Wars
for victims of the black blade

That draws forth red blood
to feed insatiable gods.

Buckled by these lies,
their empire spread and spread

Till those it stifled
rose and joined its enemies.

Then the Spaniards burned
all those codices as well.

trustee

the cursus honorum of small south texas
towns—as a kid he works in minnesota
fields. the grueling and endless labor, the
overseers fostering greed and speed while
quashing cooperation teach him things:
he learns to mistrust los gringos, learns
the rule of no seas pendejo, screw or get
screwed, family first, laws are obstacles.

back in the rio grande valley late each fall
he helps his dad with odd construction jobs
and attends classes that have no relevance,
dreary, droning lectures, empty and galling.
he drops out to get his CDL, wrangling a rig
for don pepe for a few years, saving up for
his own. then a dangerous haul through the
falfurrias checkpoint leaves him ten thousand
bucks richer and smiled upon by cartel saints.

he marries, sires six, building up his own
company truck by truck, haul by haul, bribe
after mordida after handshake. his kids
enter school, and he begins to pay attention
to board elections, finds candidates in need
of funds, willing to reciprocate. his wife takes
up the mantle of community organizer, of
politiquera. they get their guys elected,
and contracts are inked, kick-backs given,
relatives discretely hired. in four more years,
he is ready, runs on a ticket with the other
team (the only loyalty is to family, familia).

he wins. immediate influence, power, lana:
money sheared like wool from those sheep.
watches as judges, sheriffs, commissioners
fall to aggressive federal oversight. laughs.
not me. no soy pendejo. grand jury soon
starts snooping, and district personnel, heads
of departments, cabinet members, are in

the sights of the fbi. suspensions, arrests,
monitor from the texas education agency.

pressure is on, but he feels invincible. not
me. driver scheduled to run 1200 pounds
of pot north gets sick. he has to take care
of the situation personally, decides to drive
the load himself. distracted by phone, runs
a red light. dps officer searches, finds drugs.
million-dollar bond. they'll take care of his
family. he'll do the time and then assume
a less public role, for he is in. you stay in.
because who can you trust outside, really?

A thing enskied

A life of tribulation and poverty
had scoured her free of pretense,

and she wore her contradictions
like proud bruises or scars, a cigarette

in mahogany fingers, smoke curling
past flashing eyes, an angel perhaps

or something more ancient, awful—
a tzitzimitl, meant to be adored

and feared, all black plumes and
talons and squirming serpents.

I almost dropped to my knees when
that unspeakable gaze fell on me, then

she cocked her night-dark head, smiled
at so instantly devout an acolyte—

such an easy thing to tear out
my heart and place it in her claws.

Tessitura

That's my problem, I told the editor—my voice
wants to wander the spectrum, whispering
nervous anecdotes and febrile dreams before
launching into a sermon full of beatitudes and
metonymic brimstone. It wants to croon romance
and bellow rolling, dactylic waves of war. Raspy
and twangy and aspirating aitches with Latino
limberness, it glissades over technobabble and
extraterrestrial names, hewing close to the real
then mixing in harmonics of magic, rumbling
ultra-low frequencies that raise goose bumps,
making bones rattle and stomachs flop in horror.

He ranted in his monotone, wise to the industry,
cautioned me to not confuse the reader, to be
predictable, to find my range and work it well,
but I was already trying out a gleeful falsetto
that best fit the contours of the next words.

La gente en junio
a dokugin hankasen

Barrios are teeming,
alive with raucous laughter—
summer has begun.

Sallow face at a window—
la vecina, phone in hand.

The raspa man comes
pushing his broken-down cart—
kids flock for snow cones.

Comadres in housecoats chat
beside the sidewalk, brooms poised.

And there's la güera,
walking to the store with an
entourage of boys.

Don Mario stands watching as
El Maistro stuccoes his house.

Doña Petra kneels
amidst her blue mistflowers,
crowned with butterflies.

In the placita, old men
play dominoes, reminisce.

The next street is blocked
to serve the loud World Cup dreams
of young soccer stars.

Smiling priests—one Mexican,
one Chinese—visit widows.

Alone in his room,
unbeknownst to anyone,
el Licenciado has died.

El Tuerto Guzmán slips weed
into a customer's hand.

Locked in for the day,
five-year-old Flora awaits
her working mother.

Amidst shady mesquites,
Sara reads fate in your palm.

Mr. Cruz, "el Sir,"
nurses the first hangover
of his break from kids.

Tangled in hand-me-down sheets,
newlyweds make hungry love.

Los Sánchez pile thick
into the family Bronco—
the ocean beckons

And the splendor of the sun
will illuminate the way.

Iteration

The crazy one, beautiful and blonde, first kiss and stepmom at gunpoint,
    boarding school eroding the summer romance into memories;
The sweet and good one, tall and honest, undeserved, against whom I
    committed my first betrayal, leaving unicorns in my wake;
The sexy neighbor, like a siren, forbidden fruit, who dragged me into
    the depths of my own darkness and left me drowning;
The LDS German, who wrote *ich liebe dich* on my trapper keeper but
    who said we could never be sealed, so what was the point;
The big-hipped beauty with hands larger than mine, whose smile was
    like the sun, even though my eyes sought darkness;
The bunny who wanted to kiss and kiss and kiss, everywhere, in front
    of everyone, all the time, till I grew unexpectedly weary;
The girl with cornrows, whose hand I held for a day before her friends
    and brothers vetoed the interracial fling;
The skinny one with braces who let me feel her breasts;
The one they called Peanut, young and brown and goofy as hell;
The tomboy, her legs glowing with golden peach fuzz;
The poolside queen, whose boyfriend chased me into the woods, where
    I tripped like every victim in every horror movie ever made;
The organist's daughter, round owl glasses and pure soul, the first time
    failed love became everlasting friendship;
The literate, diminutive Catholic with whom I attended my first mass,
    butterfly kisses of Italian and Yucatec extraction;
The Chicana metal head with golden teeth who ground eager fingers
    into my flesh, black nails leaving red lunettes;
The haughty one with cold eyes and black curls;
Her younger sister, whom I dated out of spite;
The odd and funny girl with her fine webbing of scars, upon whose bed
    I learned the ineluctable pull of that particular hunger;
The tall Baptist who borrowed the only copy of the first book I wrote
    and never gave it back, like precious jewelry after a break-up;
Ah, and the green-eyed track star, with her prog rock and love of pink,
    who bound me to her, heart and soul, friendship yearning
    toward some febrile light, the taste of her lips, the scent of her
    flesh, the feel of her opening to my touch ... and the sickening
    realization that she would not be mine, refused to make formal
    our bond out of a need for a different sort of man, gritty and
    sturdy and dangerous, not the elven poet with wistful eyes
and hollow bones;

Then the artist and model, passionate yet empty, needing to be filled
        and filled and filled so that when I had nothing more to pour
        from myself into that delicious chocolate flesh that arced and
        groan and cried, she dissolved into the darkness of oblivion
        and I went even deeper, down into the abyss itself;
The strange and startling surprise, a young man's hand in the predawn
gloom that awakened me to the fullness of my identity;
And that was what brought me here, the road wending through
        all those hearts, the journey that set me at your feet:
Not a kiss do I regret, not a wound would I undo;
I am the sort of man I am because of every one of them.

Tzompantli

In rows, like putrid gourds
Or jack-o'-lanterns black with rot,
The minds they yield are arranged
By blood-tipped fingers
That spider over gelatinous masses of ruin.
Whispering ritually, she kisses each
And gives a pious bow.
Those men won the game,
Earned their prize,
Paid the price—
Noble opponents for whom her flesh
Was worth the soul's destruction.

Lovely Thing

Lovely thing that dances at the edge,
Heedless of the masses' cries:
Straddle the rift betwixt left and right—
Moderate, rational, sane.

Wander the valley of endless now
Shadowed by looming future and past;
Skirt the boundaries of militant gender—
Search for androgynous gray.

Ashen Boy

O ashen boy who's fled this world
A father I'd have been to you,
Dear elder brother for my son,
Companion for my daughter's soul.

I knew you came from monstrous folk—
Harpies, vampires, succubi—
But I believed that you could change,
That you could turn your noble back
On ancient gold once bought with blood.

I was deceived, and by my fault
Your claws curled into bitter fists
That beat my sweet and precious girl
As venom pumped along those veins
You chose to open to the dark,
Your voice gone hoarse with howling.

Perhaps I could have given more
To aid you in your quest to be
A goodly man, but one child
Was sacrifice enough, I swore.
I drove you from my home.

For I could see the smoking
Of your hell-hot demon heart,
Which had burnt your soul to ash
Long before this crematorium
Could feed on your cold flesh.

Yet know this, ashen boy,
Whatever darkness you now roam:
There was a time I loved you well
And I weep to know you gone.

Nepantlero

birthed at the intersection
atheistic shaman, harbinger of zero
Spanish-speaking freckled güero
spinning literary genre tales
over tribal beats and electric guitars
blubbering and logical, vicious though kind
food stamps, housing and Kundera
Santo, Star Trek, Scorsese, Bogie
Shakespeare, Cervantes, Paz
Christ-Buddha-Quetzalcoatl embracing
Satan-Mara-Tezcatlipoca under the gaze
of Tonantzin-Kali-Gaia-Holy Ghost
syncretic and paradoxical osculation
white trash and blue-collar Chicano
identity burst again and again
rebuilt like a kludgy mosaic
with bits of this culture and that
gender as fluid as feels good
everywhere and nowhere at once
oncān, tētzalan tēnepantlah, in nepantlahtli—
liminal limbo from which to watch it all
everyone's fragile reality
both real and unreal
all true and yet false
like an image floating
on a still, dark pool
in the womb
of the earth
before the
wyrms
rise.

Crossing the Threshold

Awakening to the Moon

Formless whorls of light
swell and ebb in dreams
marching close then slipping
away till, in a limbo edging
wakefulness, the argentine
abstraction contracts into
a bright sphere that streams
its cold, hard illumination
through the window.

In this mythic frontier between
oneiric and empiric realms
it is never clear how the cowardly
god, false arrogance dimmed by
a rabbit's feet, became the defiant
woman, her head hurled into
the heavens: whatever its source,
that slaty glare shimmers askew
upon the still, silent world,
mute and menacing.

Potter at Chaco
Pueblo potter, 700 C.E.

The white clay slick beneath my palms,
I shape a jar in which to store precious water
so scarce in these times of drought
that draw the People tight within our canyon.

From this narrow cliffside terrace
I see smoke wreathing from a kiva,
just as our ancestors emerged from their sipapu,
fleeing the Underworld to shape a homeland.

Their spirits take my hands now, guide them
as the vessel spirals thin and tall.
Once heat has baked it hard, I will add sacred designs
to honor their wisdom—ineffable angles and turns.

Then my husband—our wares nestled
in a net upon his sturdy back—will bear it up
the Great North Road, trading in a village far away
for food, perhaps a lovely stone or feather, too.

Somewhere, days hence, unknown lips
will receive a gift of cool and vital water
from my distant, thoughtful fingers,
kiss the edges I now taper.

The Binding of the Years

Our grandfathers warned us—
Every fifty-two years
The turning of great cosmic wheels
Brings the two calendars,
Sacred and solar,
Back into alignment.
A perilous time, this changing of cycles:
The universe unstable
For five nameless days,
Time enough to snuff the sun,
Time enough for demons
To drop from the stars
And devour the sea-ringed world.

The old ones found a way
To stave off apocalypse—
They ceased their laboring,
Performed ablutions,
Fasted and prayed and
Drew blood from their flesh.
Everything old in the home was destroyed:
Crockery, clothing, footwear and mats.
All fires were extinguished.
Silence fell across the land.

On the final day of the cycle,
The priests of the holy flame
Marched east from Tenochtitlan
To a temple platform perched
Upon a dead volcano.
There, as the sun set perhaps forever,
They sacrificed a man
And drilled new fire to life
In his hollowed chest.

Thus were the former years bound,
A new calendar round begun.
The flames were fed into a bonfire
That lit bright torches

To be carried to every temple
So holy hearths might be quickened
And feed each family's private coals—
Ten thousand glowing point of hope
Infusing the sun with energy
Till the first dawn of a new year
Splintered the eastern dark.

Three Aztec Kings, Cocooned

Moctezuma I
History envelopes me as I stand upon this mount,
Tight-fitting and slick like the sacrificial skin
I once donned for a month as a young warrior.
I stretch forth a sheathed arm and empire swells,
Consuming the high plains like fire hissed
From the mouth of Huitzilopochtli, god of war,
Whose regalia encases me, immersing this man
In the destiny he spun down the years, howling spirals
Like vast, woofy sandstorms that prowl the deserts,
Those dunes my fathers crossed to find their home.

Ahuizotl
About me curls the roiling smoke,
Billowing black from the scorched battlefield.
I pull my cloak tight around my avid flesh
And stride amidst the cloying attar of blood
Spilled in tremulous libation to the sun,
Whose light enfolds and nurtures us all.
Though young, I feel the weight of this duty
Squeeze my heart like a vise: the cogs of the cosmos
Must be greased with the viscera of the valiant,
And so I rain death upon my enemies
And steal away their bravest men.
When I return to our jade-circled city,
The praise of my people will surge like the tide
As I ascend the temple steps, a whirling current
That cradles the triton they call king.

Nezahualcoyotl
I close my eyes and the steady tattoo of the drums
Becomes the beating of massive wings,
And the Giver of Life wheels through the sky,
Spiraling down toward the city I raised in his name.
I feel those gorgeous plumes enfold me,
Drawing me close to the divine, and his song begins.
Oh, hear that trilling melody, my friends!
It whirls about the world like garlanded blooms,
Calling us ever homeward, to that distant shore

Where dewy mists forever shroud
The souls of worthy warriors.

Aztlan Abandoned

Note: According to the Mexica—the Nahua tribe we now call Aztecs—their ancestors emerged a thousand years ago from Aztlan, their name for the US Southwest, guided by the god Huitzilopochtli. During this exodus from the clutches of cruel overlords, Huitzilopochtli left the Mexica for a time under the leadership of his sister Malinalxochitl, a powerful sorceress with very different plans for their people than what her warring brother envisioned.

Across the white dunes the Mexica wend
Like a river of souls through the desert,
And my brother—doughty mage, demi-god,
Bright hummingbird leading them south—
Pauses at their head, arms lifted to the sun,
In ecstatic trance at the edge of Aztlan.

Returning to himself, he gathers together
The chiefs of each clan. "Fathers," he cries,
"I must leave you for a time. My sister,
Malinalxochitl, will care for your needs
While alone I seek the gods' counsel."
Those elders balk and beat their chests.

"No, Lord Huitzilpochtli! We trust not
That haughty witch and her strange cult
To Quilaztli, goddess of cradle and snake."
But my brother says nothing more—
He simply strides off into a mirage,
In search of power and destiny.

As the clans camp on crests and slacks,
I gather my tlatlahuihpochtin, luminous tribe.
Burning scorpions and spiders and sage,
We scry the smoke for signs of pursuit
From the cruel overlords of the arid steppes
And creosote brush land that we've escaped.

My auguries speak clear truth—we are free,
No need to rush foolhardy and afraid
Past the Great River. Days grow into weeks,

And there is no sign of Huitzilopochtli.
So I take my place on the mat of authority,
Speak our future at the heart of that vast erg.

"Our exodus has ended. Here we shall remain.
I shall teach you to draw austere bounty
And water from the hostile bosom
Of this cactus-studded desert. No more
Will you spill human blood to appease
The gods. Colder ichor will suffice."

In time they learn my ways, grudging,
And we carve out a sliver of homeland.
Bright-hued tents spread like rainbow waves
Across the sea of dunes. Snakes and toads
Are sacrificed to Quilaztli. Peace holds,
Redoubled by spells and obedient bugs.

Until my brother returns, face smeared
With foreign blood, skin bronzed by the sun.
"South," he commands, voice low and raw.
"I am returned with arrow and a shield,
For battle is our work. Conquest awaits.
Abandon your tents, fools. We must away!"

I begin to protest. He waves me mute with magic.
"Who stands with this drinker of serpent bile,
This hierophant of sand who whispers arcane hexes
To centipedes and termites? Who would stay,
Awaiting enslavement?" My tribe enfolds me,
Joined by a hundred others, faithful few.

Clenching his fist, he drops us into sleep.
We awaken to find ourselves alone on the sand,
Abandoned, stripped of provisions. Yet I smile,
For we have shrugged off that tyrant's yoke as well.
Now we too will forge a nation—not by conquest,
But with enlightened minds, bleached desert lore
And Our Mother's undying, reptilian love.

Pausing to Gaze upon Death's Bleak Spoor

her body quiescent, the ravages of time
smoothed by the snapping of life's tense
wires. Cold fury settles deeper in my chest
as I resume my trudging forward along this
darkling and merciless path. Specters crowd
the margins, silent eyes observing, waiting.
Ahead, that gaunt and black-shrouded back
is barely visible in the mist and fading light.
I quicken my pace. Like every man, one day
I will overtake that thieving fiend, that blight
of joy and love. I hold no bootless hope of
victory, but I will strive there upon the brink,
smashing my futile fists against his ivory
to repay every unspeakable loss
before he shuts my eyes at last.

Marigolds

Marigolds twisting
In ivory fingers
Turquoise stripes
Speckled crimson

Powdered petals
The faces of victims
Torrents of rain
Offered the dead

Stare at the dregs
Yellow skirts spinning
Hallucination
Insects that flee

Catrina calls you
Godmother Death
Sphere and sickle
Skulls and hands

Four long years
Razors and jaguars
Bat-black darkness
Howling wind

The center opens
Dazzling white
Amid marigold garlands
You are home at last

Crow, Buzzard and Hummingbirds

Crow was in trouble. Thoughtless and arrogant,
He had blundered into Buzzard's demesne,
The vast, bony desert where moribund mammals
Surrender themselves to heat, sand and beak.

Buzzard watched him from thorny green heights,
Jaundiced eyes glowering, two rotten suns,
And when Crow fluttered down upon a bloated corpse,
The scavenger spread its ragged wings to spiral close.

Startled into fluttering black by the feel of talons,
Crow couldn't twist the tarnished coil of his body:
His sable beak was pressed into dead flesh
As rapier pecking pierced his ancient hide.

Unaccountably, a charm of hummingbirds,
Blue-green blur of thrum and whistle,
Streamed by like filtered liquid sunlight,
Redolent of popcorn flowers and pulsing with joy.

Buzzard, startled, loosened its avid grip,
And Crow flipped onto his back, clawing
At the scavenger's belly, snapping at its wings,
Dismembering the fiend in a few fierce seconds.

Crow stood and watched the hummingbirds
As they swooped at blooming cactus arms.
"I want a tribe like that," he cried. "I want a flock
That will move as I move, think as I think!"

He looked about at the chunks of steaming flesh:
An idea wormed its way out of his nut-like brain.
Yanking plumes from his own black breast,
He planted each in a bloody bit of Buzzard.

Crow spat on the chunks, cawed himself hoarse,
Rolled them together and squatted down
Like a female warming her precious eggs
Until beneath him came a squirming chirp.

Soon six black fledglings were begging for food
And Crow slipped them slivers of bitter bird.
Laughing, he thought of the mischief they'd cause,
"A murder I'll call us, to mark our start."

outside the earthborn brain

nature red in tooth and claw
hisses hot breath against our
skin—glittering eyes in the dark
and distant yet ominous howls.

storms and drought and flood,
shuddering earth and raging
fire—life in danger even from
enemies too small for us to see.

and somehow this bleakness
cannot suffice, cannot explain
the terror curling in our minds,
the surety that monsters roam.

so we scour forest and desert,
trawl the rivers, dredge the lakes,
scry the heavens with ear and
eye, desperate for tracks, signs.

demons there must be. ghosts.
aliens. incomprehensible gods.
something. intolerable that we
ourselves are the only monsters.

And on the mere the wailing died away

What artifact, then, slips into the sea?
Raft of serpents? Sword of sun-lit steel?
Crumbling castles, mayhap, or pyramids.
Cities that crack and slide like glaciers
Into rising tides of avid entropy.
Or vaster still—noetic skeins,
Empathic threads unraveling,
Hope fading to a spot,
Dark and formless
On the horizon.

Malinalli Steps into the Gap

Then comes the moment
that Malinalli—freshly christened
"Marina," clearly a sign from the gods,
receiving a name from a foreign priest
that so echoes her day sign—
after several days on the floating castle
hears one of the princes who have just boarded
and who cannot speak Mayan to Father Aguilar
ask in Nahuatl "Who speaks for your people?"

It is a crux, a breach, a pivot, this moment.
She sees that clearly. Neither group
understands the other. Tensions mount.
Malinalli envisions the disastrous outcome—
the oppressive regime of Tenochtitlan
will use the confusion and conflict
to consolidate power, ally even with enemies
to drive the newcomers away. These are men,
after all, proud and violent and rash,
like those who have hurt her again and again.

Yet history or fate has forged a lever,
and though her heart races with hidden fear,
Malinalli steps into the gap. "My lord,"
she boldly calls, "the gentleman you seek
stands over there, apart from the others."
She points to Cortés. Aguilar turns to her, stuttering
stilted Mayan. "Marina, do you speak their language?"
"Yes, reverend priest. I learned it as a child.
It is the language of the Emperor and his people."

The foreign priest informs his captain.
Cortés calls Malinalli to his side. "From now on
you are my tongue, do you understand?"
he tells her through Aguilar. "Like this priest,
you must be ever at my side." And before the wheels
of time can turn, she feels the rough hands of destiny
seize her willing soul and thrust against the fulcrum.

Night Axe

Young Cihtli rose at 3 am to sweep the temple portico
while priests descended to a spring to mortify their flesh.
She watched them leave as one and then return alone
with ragged, bloody ears, with wounded tongues and arms—
thus consecrated to their rites were they as she to hers,
sealed in a mountain cloister above the city of Tetzcohco.

That morning, though, two came rushing up the path,
long hair disheveled, eyes wide with fright, no mutilation.
"Inside!" they shouted, pushing Cihtli and their other charges,
children of nobles, a measure of families' devotion to the gods.
"We have heard a thudding sound, like the thwack of arrows
in sturdy pines, again and again. The Night Axe is upon us!"

But Cihtli knew of that ghoul: her older brothers had told her
the tale. Now both were dead, led into frivolous battle
by the new king, Cacamatzin, mere puppet of the Mexica,
of their self-styled emperor, Moteuczoma. Lips curled with hate,
the girl cast aside her broom, and slipping past the startled priests,
she dashed away into the darkness of the haunted woods

The blows echoed hard and loud, like axes biting into snowy firs,
and Cihtli grimaced, eager to wield the dreadful portent herself.
She left the well-worn trail, stood stock still in a clearing, waited.
Before too long, the apparition lumbered into view, lit silver
by the meager moon. Like a man it seemed, though headless,
its torso sliced from belly to neck, rib cage pulled apart like doors.

Those slabs of flesh swung open and shut with a horrid thud
every time the Night Axe took a shambling step, like a maw
flapping in ravenous oblivion. When its chest gaped wide,
the girl could glimpse its black and silent heart, dangling there.
Blood ringing in her ears, she waited till it was upon her at last,
then Cihtli reached in and seized that rotted lump, ripping it free.

As quick as she could, she rushed away, never looking back.
In the temple garden, she dropped to her knees, wrapped it
tightly in her sash and buried the heart deep in the fertile soil.

The girl would not explain her actions. She was punished.
But in the morning, she dug up her boon, finding white feathers
in its place. Propitious sign. The gods approved. Cihtli smiled.

A few days later came the news: huge mansions, floating
on the sea; armored deer that bore pale, bearded men;
spear-throwers that launched stones and fire and smoke.
The girl would have her revenge. She would see them fall,
those former mercenaries, usurpers of the Toltec Way.
She imagined her fingers, curling 'round the handle of an axe.

Gonzalo Guerrero

The caravel shipwrecked, you rescued
as many as you could, your lifeboat drifting
for two weeks along the Yucatan coast,
no food or drink beyond dwindling piss.

Your weakness shamed you when, beached,
the survivors and you were handily caught
by the small, dark natives. Some of the men
were slaughtered in sacrifice to strange gods.

The rest of you, first Europeans to set foot in
Mesoamerica, were caged. The women succumbed
to disease and despair. You and the priest,
Aguilar, conspired a bootless escape. Most died.

Running through the jungle, you were overtaken
by slavers. Through the familiar savagery
of the marketplace, your valuable flesh
made its way to the realm of Xaman Ha'.

What compelled you—Catholic soldier who helped
drive the Moors from Spain, who arrived in
the New World to quash internecine squabbles—
to embrace an alien culture and faith?

Was it self-preservation that led you to reveal
military techniques, to render yourself invaluable
as the warriors of King Taxmar carried out
campaigns made more successful by your aid?

When you were given to King Nachan Can
of Ch'aak Temal, you rescued his general
from a caiman's deadly jaws and thereby won
not only your freedom, but also a warrior's rank.

The wheels of the calendars, of the cosmos, turn
and turn. Eight ceremonial years later, invader Cortés
learned that two Spaniards lived among the Maya.
He rescued Father Aguilar, sent him to find you.

Ah, but you had changed, had you not? You loomed
over the priest, face tattooed, ears and lip pierced,
your wife at your side—Princess Zazil Ha', haughty
daughter of Nachan Can, she whose love converted you.

"Brother Aguilar," you muttered in halting Spanish,
"How can you ask me to leave? I am married now,
father of three beautiful children. To these people
I am a great captain of war, part and parcel of the realm.

"Do you not see me, priest? Imagine this altered form
there before your fellow Spaniards. They would take
me for a savage. No, give me some bright green beads,
and I will pass them to my children as gifts from home."

Then Zazil Ha', understanding the gist of the exchange,
spat in disdain. "Husband, how dare this slave come
before you to address you in this way? Let him be gone
at once, taking with him such foolish notions!"

Yet Aguilar made one last attempt: "Remember, Gonzalo,
that you are a Christian. Do not condemn your soul
for the sake of a simple Indian girl. If she and your
children worry you so, bring them with you, soldier."

But you were no longer a Christian, were you? No,
you now walked the Green Road, laid in the beginning
by gods older than Christ, and you refused to be
deceived or diverted, would not stumble or fall away.

For twenty solar years you taught your adopted folk
to fight against Spanish might, pushing that army
again and again from Yucatan, till you finally fell,
blasted by a harquebus while defending Ticamaya.

You lay dead on the battlefield all night, surrounded
by loyal men who had followed you into death, stars
wheeling overhead till the Milky Way, that glowing
road to Xibalba, led your noble soul into the afterlife.

In the morning your sons, the first mestizos in Mexico,
gathered up your empty flesh and set you afloat
upon the Ulúa River, which swept your corpse down
into the vast ocean whence it had once emerged.

But the best part of you, Gonzalo Guerrero, lingers
in this fertile soil—your love of the Ma'ya'ab, land
of the few, where you merged Cross and World Tree,

Mother of God and Goddess, sword and spear,
Eucharist and sacrifice, sea and cenote, your
loyal heart and ours—Founder, Father, Friend.

In Huehca Ohtli—The Deep Road
Nahuatl poems from the time of quarantine

1
monacaztlapoh
moyōllohtlapoh
motlapoh īhuān
quichtacanōnōtz
in cemānāhuatl

she opened her ears
opened her heart
opened herself—
and the universe
whispered to her.

2
micqui quimichin
nemactli zacapan—
nēchtlacualtia nomiztōn

dead field mouse
gift upon the green grass—
my cat brings me food.

3
ihcuāc tēmiquiz
cuix in tēmiquiz?
cātleimeh in ehēcameh
quihuālittaz inoc cochiz?

when she dreams
is it someone's death?
which of those wispy ghosts
will come visit while she sleeps?

4
inic titlachīhuazqueh
monequi titlapolōzqueh
quimilhuilih in Yohualtzin
in īcōāuhtzin—
Ihhuitica Ehēcatzin.
zan nēn huetzi
in mēlcihcihuiliz
in mochōquiliz.

in order to create
we must destroy
said the Night
to his twin—
the Feathered Wind.
you sigh
you weep
in vain.

ahmo, quihtoh
inōn Quetzalli,
in ihcuāc ehēcaz
īhuān quiyahuiloz
quimatiz in tlācatl
in tlazohtlalo īhuān
nīnetemachīl niyez.

no, replied that
Precious Plume,
when the breeze blows soft
and rain cools their skin
folks will know
they are loved
and feel hope.

5
cāctimani in āltepēmeh
tepāmpan tēmih
in cōcomīxtin
ohtlica zacaixhua
ācalohtēnco quih
chipāhuac ātl
in māmazāh auh
nāltic ehcatl īpan
patlānih in tōtōmeh.

zatepan tiquīzah
ye tiquimatih in
ahmo tāqueh.

in the silent cities
lizards teem the walls
grass sprouts
upon the roads
deer drink deep
from canals
that run clear
and birds glide
upon the fresh air.

we emerge at last
to find we hardly
matter.

6
ahcic in xōpaniztli
yeceh nocalco nicatca
inic ahmo nēchahcic
īmahpil xopalectic.

spring arrived, but I
was inside my house
so her verdant fingers
couldn't curl around me.

7
calāmpa, chachalacah
in chachalacahqueh,
pāquiliztica quimolhuiah
in quēnin tēpēhuazqueh

outside, the chachalacas
chatter, cheerily conspiring
to retake the world.

8
ye quiyahui
in ācitlālin
quinxiuhcaltia
mochintin.

rain falls
pearling
the world
greener.

9
quēnoqueh mopochīnaz
in tēicnīuhyōtl īxquichica
in huel tiquihtoāz,
"ca ic ōquīz,
ic ōtēchtlalcahuih
in cocoliztli".

I wonder how far
society will unravel
before we can say
"that's how it ended,
that's how the virus
finally left us."

10
ye tlatlatzini,	thunder rolls
ahcualli tētzāhuitl–	like a portent of doom
nicochiznequi.	and I grow drowsy.

11
in tenāmitl	no walls
in huēyi ātl	or seas
ahmo huel	could
quiyacānāmictih	stop
in ahittoni	the invisible
tēpoloāni.	invader

12
notēnco nihcac	at the edge of myself
īhuān niquitta	I stand and behold
in huehca ohtli	the deep road
niman ihīyōtica	then with a sigh
centlani nicalaqui.	I enter the abyss

13
zan cuepōni	the cocoon
in calocuilin	just bursts
patlānquīza	out flies
xōchicuīcatl	poetry

14
mizquitzalan	among the mesquites
īntlan nicnīhuān	with my cousins
ticcuah ītlaaquīllo	eating the pods–
titōnalmīyohqueh.	striped by sunbeams.

15
niquinilnāmiqui	I keep thinking of
in Cōāhuiltēcah	the Coahuiltecans
in Huēyipōl Ātōyātl	living on the banks
iātēnco nemihqueh	of the Rio Grande
īhuān quicuahqueh	eating fish, deer
mīmichtin, māmazāh,	anacahuita jelly on
in īxōcotzopēlic	mesquite tortillas

in āmacuahuitl
motehtēca īpan
mizquitlaxcalli
inoc īntahtzin in tōnatiuh
īnnāntzin in tlālticpactli
quinnāhuatequihqueh,
īmātzin tlanēxtiāni
īhuān nemōhuani.

while father sun
and mother earth
held them tight
with arms of light
and verdant life.

16
ōmpa xālpan
īmmachiyo āyōmichin
ātezcapan
āpopohti in ācuetzpalin
zan nocallān
motēcah in huēyi ātl,
in cuahuitl, in tēpemeh.
niman ōmotzauc
in cuāxōchtli—
quēxquich cāhuitl
in huel niquittaz
nochān Tzapotlān?

turtle tracks
upon the sand
crocs floating
in the lagoon
a home flanked
by ocean, jungle,
sloping foothills.
but they've closed
the border now—
how long till I
see my magical
Zapotal again?

17
cēhuilōni ītzintlān
in mizquitl ehcauhyoh—
ca zan noteōcal.

a chair beneath
the shady mesquite—
my only church.

18
ītloc xococuahuitl
māzcapōtzaltia—
moyēcchīhua
in tlāllōtl.

anthills rising
round invasive orange trees—
the earth seeks balance

19
ayāc
mictlān
iuhqui
inic
huehcāhuani
in pilchiyaliztli.

no hell
as eternal
as waiting
for one's children
to arrive.

20
ye nicān
mictlāmpa
teuhtlālpampa
tlein huel
quichīhuazqueh
in noxhuihuān?

right here in
the Dead North
this desiccated land
what will my
grandchildren
be able to build?

21
huitztlah teuhtlah—
intla huel nicmatizquia
ītlahtol in tlatōctli omitl.

dusty brushland—
if only I could understand
the whispering bones below.

22
cuauhpītza in āehēcatl
mopechoa in mizquitl—
teōxōpancuīcatl.

warm Gulf wind whistles
through bowing mesquite—
holy song of spring.

23
in cāctoc ohtli īpan
tlein ahihtōlōni
tlācatchiya?

upon these silent streets
what unspeakable thing
waits to be born?

24
mācahcapāni nochpōch—
tēchchīhuilia in ticalaquiloh
īnnexōchipolōliz tochichicahuān.

my daughter pats out nokake—
ancestral treats
for a trapped family.

25
huehcāhua zānīlli—
ētlamantin nocotocyōhuān,
nopīlhuān nēchilhuiah.

long chat with my kids—
three parts of my soul
all speaking to me out loud.

26
ahmo tēmāma
iuhqui tlahtoāni—
zan centlamāmalli in cuitlatl

does not carry his people
on his back like a king—
just a load of shit.

27
ā, in tlazohyōtl—
tēchīchic pozāhuac,

ah, the precious things—
lungs full of air,

tēceyaliztica neolīnīlo,
tēmātitech neahāno,
pitzōlli in papatlaca.

the freedom to move,
hands clasped tight,
a trembling kiss.

28
occeppa tlālolīni—
cuix ihza in Tepēyōllohtli?
cuix polōloz in Nāhui Olīn?

another earthquake—
is Mountain Heart awakening?
will the Fifth Sun be snuffed out?

29
quēzqui mestizo nēn quinequi
mācēhualli īpan pōhuiz—
huehcāuhtica, īpōcyo
tēpēhualiztli, tlālyōhualiztli ic
ōpoliuhqueh tomintonhuān.

how many mestizos ache
for impossible belonging—
ancestors lost to us
in the haze of conquest
and time and erasure.

30
nōncuah xiye—
zan ximocāhua mochan
xiquitta in tlālli motlatia.

keep your distance—
just stay inside your home
and watch the world burn.

31
intla ahhuel amonehuān
annemih, tinochpōch īhuān
tīnān, cāmmach huel
motlanepanilhuīz in tlācah?

if the two of you, mother and daughter,
cannot live under the same roof,
what hope is there that humanity
can ever see eye to eye?

32
zan ye tlālchipāhua
tlāllāmpa huālēhua
ītlacual in tlāltēuctli—
mā titlazohcamatinih

dawn brightens the world
and from the soil emerges
the food of Mother Earth—
let us be thankful to her.

33
tocalco, ahhuel quichīhua
in tlein quinequi, quihtoa:
"ahtitleihqueh, ahtāqueh,
intla ahtle tiquēlēhuiah,
intla ahtle tiquīxtēmoah."

at home, unable to do the things
she wants to do, she tells me:
"we are nothing, we are no one,
If we don't yearn for something,
If we don't strive to reach a goal."

34
in yancuīc totēmāuhtiliz—
cuix tēchcemmanilīz,
cuix toiyohca tiquetzaloz?

our renewed fear of others—
will it separate us futher?
will it leave us lonely and alone?

35
iz cah—
in iztāqueh
in quicuecuetlāniah
in īnyāōtlatqui:
ahcocōloh,
yōlih.

behold—
the white men
waving around
their weapons
unmolested
alive.

36
ōizcal in tiyānquiztli—
tictolpiliah in toxāyac
īhuān nēn titīxēhuiah
yehīca tiyōlahcih.

stores have reopened—
we strap on our masks
to risk our lives in vain
because we are bored.

37
in yancuīcān
ītlatzintlān
in nemiliztepētl
nihuehuetzito
ninotetextilih
iuhquin nicoyolxāuhqui,
huehcāuh nixamāntoca
niman nitlacōtōnpehpen
īhuān nicchīuh nehhuātl
in yancuīc īxyōllohtli.

the first time
I went trumbling
down the hill of life
and smashed myself
to bits at its base
like Coyolxauhqui,
I lie broken for a while
then I gathered
what pieces I could find
and built a new self.

ahmo achicualli.
oc centlamantli.
nēchnetechilpih
nociyaya, ahmo
nocnōpil, īhuān
nel quīxiptlahtic
notonal.

not better
just different.
shaped by my will,
not by accident.
a truer reflection
of my soul.

38
Māzontlān ye tlathui.
Ehēcatica cochpāna
in ohtli nopopōuh—
tlatēcpanah
quetzalcōāmeh
inic tlatzomōniz
yohualnepantlah.

Dawn breaks over Mazunte.
Brooms, aided by the wind,
sweep the streets clean—
feathered serpents order the day
for the chaos of the night.

www.ingramcontent.com/pod-product-compliance
Lightning Source LLC
Chambersburg PA
CBHW030906170426
43193CB00009BA/748